MARVELS of the USA

ACTIVITY BOOK

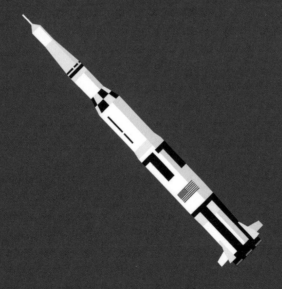

CLAIRE SAUNDERS

ILLUSTRATED BY NEIL STEVENS

Kane Miller
A DIVISION OF EDC PUBLISHING

CONTENTS

Welcome to the
MARVELS OF THE USA
ACTIVITY BOOK

The United States is packed with incredible sights—icy glaciers, steaming volcanoes, record-breaking trees, soaring skyscrapers, unique attractions, historic buildings ... and much more! As you color and puzzle your way through this activity book, you'll discover lots of fascinating facts about some of America's greatest natural wonders and man-made marvels.

First, read the fun facts on these pages, then grab your pens and pencils and dive into the activities!

If you get stuck, the answers to all the puzzles are at the back of the book.

The largest living thing on Earth is thought to be a giant honey mushroom that lives underground in Malheur National Forest in Oregon. The Humongous Fungus covers around 3.5 square miles.

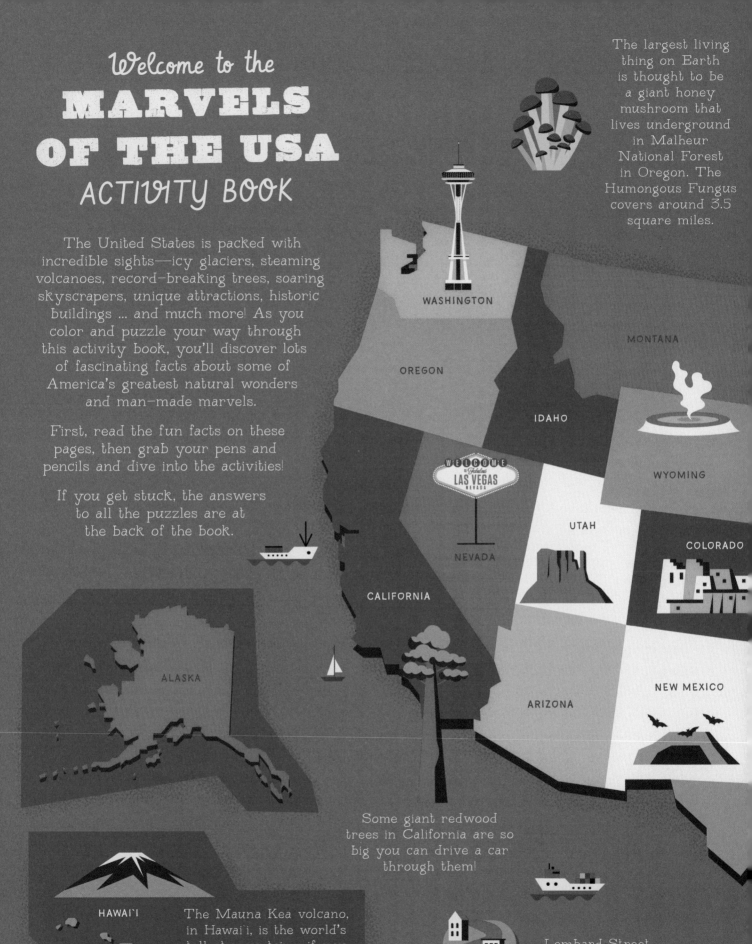

WASHINGTON

OREGON

MONTANA

IDAHO

WYOMING

WELCOME to Fabulous LAS VEGAS NEVADA

UTAH

COLORADO

NEVADA

CALIFORNIA

ARIZONA

NEW MEXICO

ALASKA

Some giant redwood trees in California are so big you can drive a car through them!

HAWAI'I

The Mauna Kea volcano, in Hawai'i, is the world's tallest mountain—if you include the part of it that's underwater. From base to top, it's almost a mile taller than Mount Everest!

Lombard Street, in San Francisco, California, holds the record for the world's most crooked street.

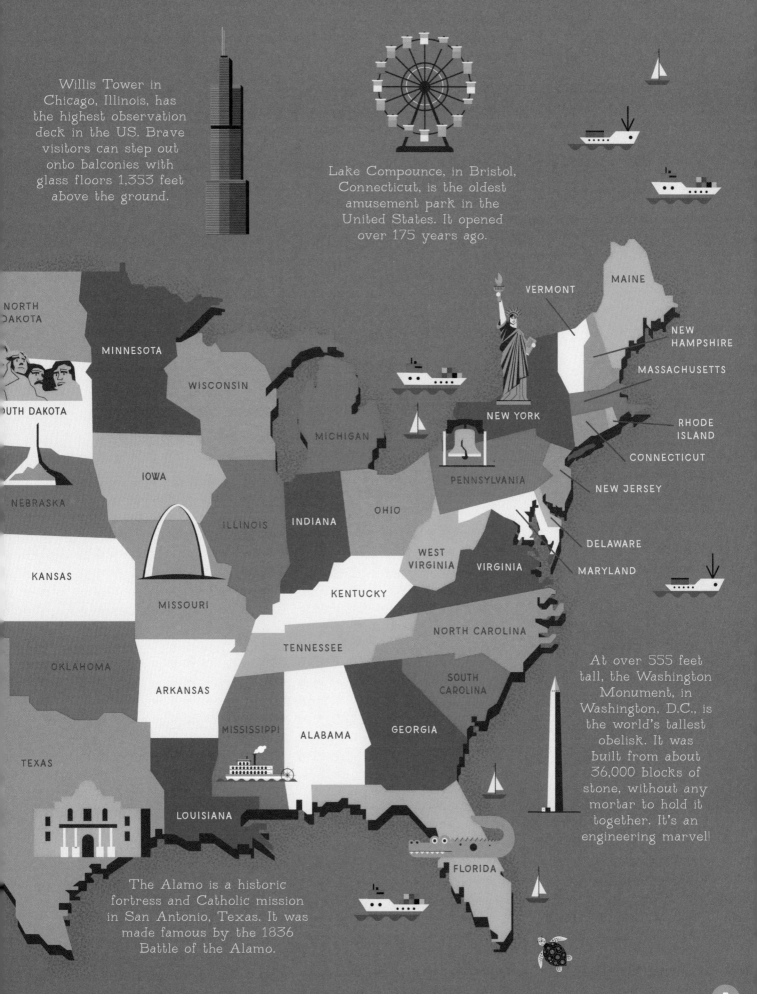

Willis Tower in Chicago, Illinois, has the highest observation deck in the US. Brave visitors can step out onto balconies with glass floors 1,353 feet above the ground.

Lake Compounce, in Bristol, Connecticut, is the oldest amusement park in the United States. It opened over 175 years ago.

NORTH DAKOTA

MINNESOTA

WISCONSIN

SOUTH DAKOTA

IOWA

MICHIGAN

NEBRASKA

ILLINOIS

INDIANA

OHIO

KANSAS

MISSOURI

KENTUCKY

WEST VIRGINIA

VIRGINIA

OKLAHOMA

ARKANSAS

TENNESSEE

NORTH CAROLINA

SOUTH CAROLINA

TEXAS

MISSISSIPPI

ALABAMA

GEORGIA

LOUISIANA

FLORIDA

VERMONT

MAINE

NEW HAMPSHIRE

MASSACHUSETTS

NEW YORK

RHODE ISLAND

CONNECTICUT

NEW JERSEY

PENNSYLVANIA

DELAWARE

MARYLAND

At over 555 feet tall, the Washington Monument, in Washington, D.C., is the world's tallest obelisk. It was built from about 36,000 blocks of stone, without any mortar to hold it together. It's an engineering marvel!

The Alamo is a historic fortress and Catholic mission in San Antonio, Texas. It was made famous by the 1836 Battle of the Alamo.

BEFORE *you get* STARTED...

This page shows just some of the awe-inspiring sights included in this book. Check the boxes of all the sights you would like to see in real life. If you have been lucky enough to see any of them already, color in the check box, too.

THE SPACE NEEDLE, WASHINGTON

THE GRAND CANYON, ARIZONA

THE WHITE HOUSE, WASHINGTON, D.C.

ALCATRAZ ISLAND, CALIFORNIA

CARLSBAD CAVERNS, NEW MEXICO

THE GATEWAY ARCH, MISSOURI

THE EVERGLADES, FLORIDA

THE STATUE OF LIBERTY, NEW YORK

GRAND CENTRAL STATION, NEW YORK

CRATER LAKE, OREGON

Write the name of your favorite place in the United States here. It can be one of the places above, or somewhere different.

WHERE AM I?

As you go through the puzzles in this book, look out for the six marvels pictured below. Once you find them, fill in the name of the state they can be found in.

CLOUD GATE

STATE: _____

MAUNA KEA OBSERVATORIES

STATE: _____

SANDY HOOK LIGHTHOUSE

STATE: _____

BILTMORE ESTATE

STATE: _____

CHIMNEY ROCK

STATE: _____

WORLD'S LARGEST BALL OF PAINT

STATE: _____

LADY OF LIBERTY

Standing in New York Harbor, the Statue of Liberty is America's most famous icon. The 151-foot-tall statue was given as a gift of friendship to the United States by France in 1884. Eager visitors can climb 354 steps to reach all the way up to the statue's crown.

Write down all of the words you can make using the letters in:

STATUE OF LIBERTY

All words must be 3 or more letters.

How did you do?

Up to 15 words: Good effort

16-29 words: Excellent

30+ words: Outstanding!

WHAT'S WRONG IN THE PARK?

Central Park is a famous 843-acre park in the middle of New York City. Over 42 million New Yorkers and tourists visit every year. In the park you can find lakes, walking paths, statues, bridges, and plenty of trees and plants.

Can you spot eight things that are wrong in this picture?

Central Park is the most filmed location in the world—around 350 movies have been filmed here.

HOT DOGS

NYC

GREAT LAKES
WORD SEARCH

The Great Lakes are a chain of five huge lakes on the US–Canada border. Together, they contain a fifth of ALL of the fresh water on Earth's surface!

Hunt through the word search to find the 16 names shown on the map: there are 2 countries, 5 lakes, 8 states, and 1 famous waterfall to find.

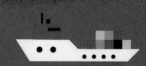

```
S B E A I S B V A O C W A A F
Q E R I W N H R O N I D T E P
E X T N D B D H Q S A O C K U
N O L A H L I I C N S S T W I
A L A V T O L O A E V N M K S
G A K L T S N C N N T E A N I
I K E Y T S D N R I A S K Y O
H E H S I W I E K R O Y W E N
C E U N W M N B T V K O P Y I
I R R N B M I C H I G A N N L
M I O E F X T O X D N E B Y L
E E N P V X B I U J J U L O I
K L A K E S U P E R I O R C S
A S L L A F A R A G A I N T C
L A K E O N T A R I O T F R D
```

Multicolor Marvel

Using the key, color in the spring's brilliant multicolored rings.

Grand Prismatic Hot Spring, in Yellowstone National Park in Wyoming, is famous for its dazzling rainbow colors. The steaming pool is larger than a football field and deeper than a 10-story building!

KEY:

1 - dark blue
2 - light blue
3 - green
4 - yellow
5 - orange
6 - brown
7 - white

The brilliant colors come from the heat-loving bacteria that live in the spring's waters.

Historic Hall

Independence Hall in Philadelphia, Pennsylvania, played an important part in US history: the Declaration of Independence was signed here in 1776. Today, visitors can take a guided tour of this historic site.

One half of the building has been drawn in the space below. Complete the picture by drawing the other, identical half, then color it in.

Don't forget to add a time to the clock!

WHICH WONDER, WHICH CITY?

THE US IS FULL OF NATURAL WONDERS, BUT THERE ARE ALSO PLENTY OF MAN-MADE WONDERS TO SEE AND ENJOY! FIVE ICONIC LANDMARKS ARE PICTURED BELOW, ALONG WITH FIVE CITY NAMES. USE THE CLUES TO HELP YOU WORK OUT WHICH LANDMARK BELONGS TO WHICH CITY.

CLUES:

THIS LANDMARK IN CHICAGO IS ALSO KNOWN AS "THE BEAN" BECAUSE OF ITS SHAPE.

THE LANDMARK IN ST. LOUIS IS AS WIDE AS IT IS TALL—630 FEET.

THE BROOKLYN BRIDGE IS NOT IN A CITY THAT BEGINS WITH THE LETTER "S."

THE SPACE NEEDLE IS IN A CITY THAT HAS 7 LETTERS.

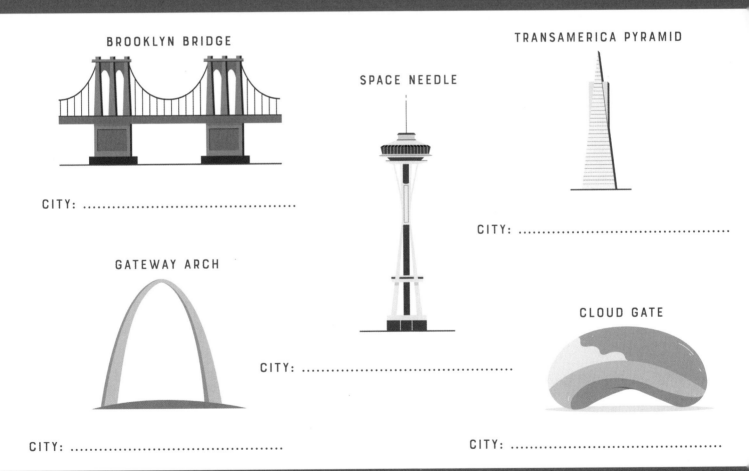

BROOKLYN BRIDGE

CITY: ....

SPACE NEEDLE

TRANSAMERICA PYRAMID

CITY: ....

GATEWAY ARCH

CITY: ....

CLOUD GATE

CITY: ....

CITY: ....

ST. LOUIS, MISSOURI

SEATTLE, WASHINGTON

SAN FRANCISCO, CALIFORNIA

CHICAGO, ILLINOIS

NEW YORK CITY, NEW YORK

CANYON
MEMORY CHALLENGE

THE GRAND CANYON, IN ARIZONA, IS ONE OF THE MOST SPECTACULAR SIGHTS ON THE PLANET—A 277-MILE-LONG, 1-MILE-DEEP GORGE, CARVED OVER TIME BY THE COLORADO RIVER. PEOPLE FROM ALL OVER VISIT THE CANYON TO TAKE IN THE VIEW, HIKE THE TRAILS, AND TRAVEL DOWN THE RIVER.

STUDY THIS PICTURE FOR ONE MINUTE. THEN COVER IT UP AND ANSWER THE QUESTIONS AT THE BOTTOM OF THE PAGE.

GRAND CANYON NATIONAL PARK IS BIGGER THAN THE ENTIRE STATE OF RHODE ISLAND!

1. WHAT COLOR IS THE HELICOPTER?

2. HOW MANY RAFTS ARE ON THE RIVER?

3. CAN YOU NAME THE THREE DIFFERENT ANIMALS IN THE PICTURE?

4. HOW MANY OF THE HIKERS ARE CHILDREN?

MOUNTAIN MAZE

Denali, in Alaska, is North America's highest peak, and the third highest in the world! It is 20,310 feet above sea level, and permanently covered in snow. Temperatures can plummet to minus 75 degrees Fahrenheit—brrr!

Help the mountaineer below find a path up the mountain, using only the even-numbered footprints.

END

90

47   16

50   8   61   32

36   21   37

4

72   43   44   75   46

22   15   68   19

5   35   10   30   54   31   97   2

98   28   57   48   56   26

41   38   64   67

24   3   91

13   27

8

57   14   95

80   85

11   22

66   START HERE

The name "Denali" means "the tall one." It comes from the Native Alaskan language Koyukon.

15

STAR ★ Statues

Many US towns and cities honor and celebrate special people (and animals!) with statues. Read about a few famous statues, then draw a statue of somebody you admire on the empty plinth.

This statue in the Kelly Ingram Park in Birmingham, Alabama, celebrates the famous civil rights leader Martin Luther King, Jr.

This statue of singer and icon Elvis Presley stands in his birth city of Tupelo, Tennessee, right outside Tupelo City Hall.

This statue of country music star Dolly Parton is found in the center of Sevierville, Tennessee, on the courthouse lawn. It's a popular stop for country music fans.

This statue of Balto the Siberian husky is found in Central Park in New York City. This heroic dog led a team of sled dogs delivering urgent medicine to sick children in Alaska in 1925.

WRITE THEIR NAME HERE

16

ROLLER COASTER RIDERS

THE US HAS HUNDREDS OF AMUSEMENT PARKS, WHERE YOU CAN FIND SOME OF THE LONGEST, TALLEST, AND FASTEST ROLLER COASTERS IN THE WORLD.

Wheeeeeee!

BELOW ARE TWO ROLLER COASTER TRACKS. COVER THE BOTTOM TRACK WITH A PIECE OF PAPER. THEN LOOK CAREFULLY AT ALL THE PEOPLE RIDING THE ROLLER COASTER ON THE TOP TRACK. AFTER 30 SECONDS, MOVE THE PAPER TO COVER THE TOP TRACK AND FOLLOW THE INSTRUCTION AT THE BOTTOM OF THE PICTURE.

CIRCLE THE FOUR EXTRA PEOPLE ON THE BOTTOM ROLLER COASTER TRACK.

The Magic Kingdom at Walt Disney World, in Florida, is the world's most visited amusement park.

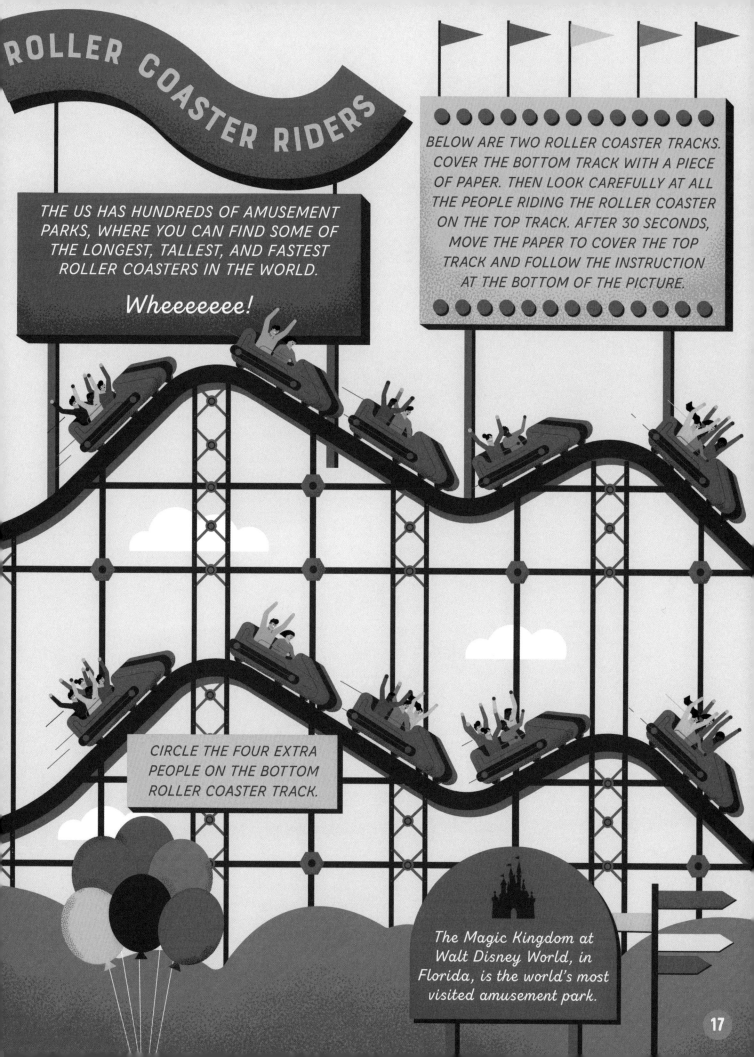

TREE
CODE
CRACKER

The US is home to BILLIONS of trees and hundreds of different species—from red maples, with leaves that turn fiery colors in the fall, to towering giant sequoias that only grow in California. Crack the codes to discover some famous and record-breaking trees. Use the tables to help you. First find the coded letter on the top row of the table—the letter below it is the answer.

1. The letters in this code have been shifted one to the right.
So, for example, "A" becomes "B," and so on.

A B C D E F G H I J K L M N O P Q R S T U V W X Y Z
B C D E F G H I J K L M N O P Q R S T U V W X Y Z A

These trees, in California's White Mountains, are the oldest living trees in the world. The oldest of them all is about 5,000 years old.

A Q H R S K D B N M D   O H M D R

_ _ _ _ _ _ _ _ _ _ _   _ _ _ _ _

2. The letters in this code have been shifted one to the left.
So, for example, "B" becomes "A," and so on.

A B C D E F G H I J K L M N O P Q R S T U V W X Y Z
Z A B C D E F G H I J K L M N O P Q R S T U V W X Y

This sequoia tree in California is the largest in the world by volume (the amount of space it takes up). It measures 102 feet around its base!

H F O F S B M   T I F S N B O

_ _ _ _ _ _ _   _ _ _ _ _ _ _

3. The letters in this code have all been shifted EITHER one to the left OR one to the right. This means there are two possible answers for each letter. Using the tables above, write down both possible answers for each letter. Then see if you can work out which letters are the correct ones! Some letters have been filled in already to help you.

This 380-foot-high redwood in California is the world's tallest tree.

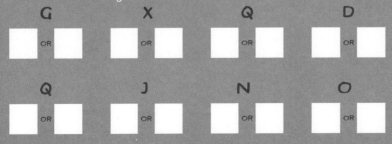

G   X   Q   D

[ ] OR [ ]   [ ] OR [ ]   [ ] OR [ ]   [ ] OR [ ]

Q   J   N   O

[ ] OR [ ]   [ ] OR [ ]   [ ] OR [ ]   [ ] OR [ ]

H _   _ P   _ R   _ _ N   ← Answer

PLANT ATTACK!

All kinds of plants grow in the United States, including some very special and rare species. The Venus flytrap is a carnivorous plant that only grows in the wild in North Carolina and South Carolina: nowhere else on the planet. When it feels an insect crawling on it, the plant snaps shut, trapping its unlucky prey inside!

Imagine you are walking in the forest and you come across a giant Venus flytrap, as big as a person. Instead of eating insects, it eats ... children! Write down what happens in the space below.

3 ... 2 ... 1 ...
LIFTOFF!

In 1969, the NASA Apollo 11 mission landed people on the moon for the very first time. The rocket that took them there was a Saturn V. A few of these mighty machines still exist today, and you can see them in three places in the US: the Kennedy Space Center in Florida; the Johnson Space Center in Houston, Texas; and the US Space & Rocket Center in Huntsville, Alabama.

Imagine you are an astronaut about to blast off into space. Where would you like to go? The moon? Mars? Or a galaxy far away? Write a postcard from your final destination.

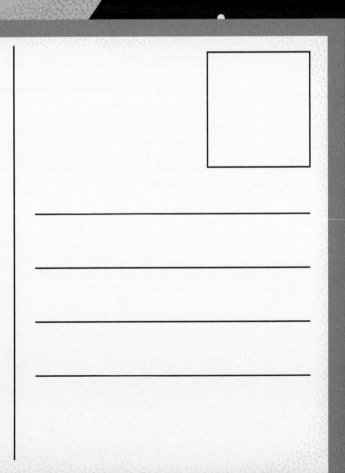

FORT KNOX MAZE

Have you heard of Fort Knox? This building in Kentucky is one of the most secure places on the whole planet! Gold bars worth billions of dollars are stored in underground vaults. Other valuable items were also stored there in the past, including the Declaration of Independence.

Imagine you have been hired by Fort Knox to test their security. Your mission is to find a way to the vault where the gold bars are stored, avoiding all the security cameras and locked gates. Good luck!

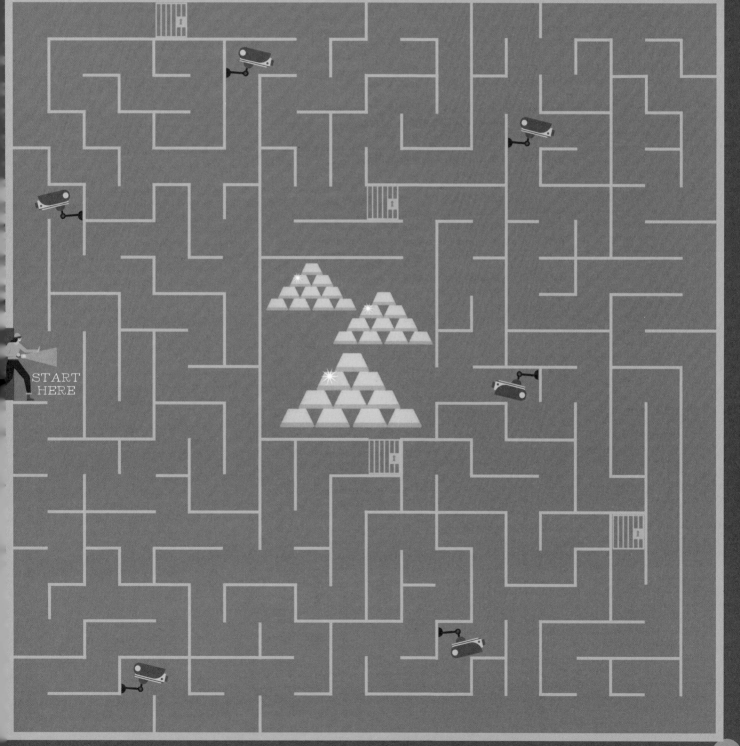

START HERE

GLACIER BAY
Hide-and-Seek

Glacier Bay in Alaska is a land of wonders: powder-blue glaciers, deep fjords, and majestic snow-topped mountains. The icy waters are home to humpback whales, harbor seals, and other animals.

A whale is hiding somewhere in this grid. Follow the instructions below to cross out squares on the grid, then draw a whale's tail on the one square that remains. Use the compass to help you.

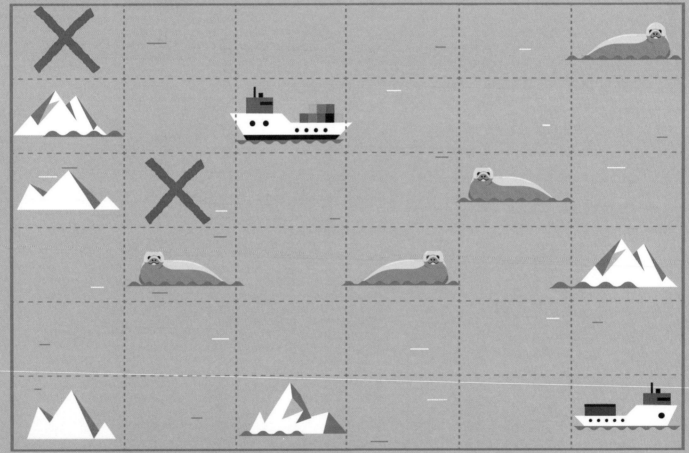

INSTRUCTIONS

- The whale is not in a square north or east of an iceberg.
- The whale is not in a square south or west of a harbor seal.
- The whale is not in a square next to a boat (above, below, left, right, or diagonal).
- Two squares are crossed off to get you started.

NIAGARA FALLS
UNSCRAMBLE

EVERY SECOND, UP TO 750,000 GALLONS OF WATER—THAT'S AROUND 15,000 BATHTUBS FULL—POUR OVER THE EDGE OF NIAGARA FALLS. THESE THREE POWERFUL WATERFALLS ARE FOUND ON THE US-CANADA BORDER. EVERY YEAR, OVER 10 MILLION PEOPLE COME TO WATCH THE WATER THUNDER DOWN.

FIND ALL OF THE LETTERS IN THE SWIRLING WATERS, AND UNSCRAMBLE THEM TO FIND THE NAME OF THE BOAT THAT TAKES TOURISTS TO THE BOTTOM OF THE FALLS. THE COLOR OF EACH LETTER TELLS YOU WHICH COLOR BOX IT BELONGS IN.

IN 1859, A DAREDEVIL KNOWN AS THE GREAT BLONDIN CROSSED NIAGARA FALLS ON A TIGHTROPE—WHILE CARRYING HIS MANAGER ON HIS BACK!

23

WHITE HOUSE QUIZ

The White House, in Washington, D.C., has been home to every president of the United States since 1800. Test your knowledge of the famous building with these multiple-choice questions.

1. WHAT SHAPE IS THE PRESIDENT'S OFFICE?

- [ ] A) Square
- [ ] B) Rectangular
- [ ] C) Oval

2. WHICH OF THESE WILL YOU NOT FIND IN THE WHITE HOUSE?

- [ ] A) Skate park
- [ ] B) Bowling alley
- [ ] C) Swimming pool

3. HOW MANY WINDOWS DOES THE WHITE HOUSE HAVE?

- [ ] A) 47
- [ ] B) 147
- [ ] C) 1,147

4. WHICH WING IS THE PRESIDENT'S OFFICE IN?

- [ ] A) East Wing
- [ ] B) West Wing
- [ ] C) North Wing

5. THE WHITE HOUSE HAS 35 WHAT?

- [ ] A) Helicopter pads
- [ ] B) Secret passageway
- [ ] C) Bathrooms

6. WHICH OF THESE PRESIDENTS NEVER LIVED IN THE WHITE HOUSE?

- [ ] A) George Washington
- [ ] B) Abraham Lincoln
- [ ] C) Barack Obama

7. WHICH OF THESE IS A FAMOUS GARDEN AT THE WHITE HOUSE?

- [ ] A) Dandelion Garden
- [ ] B) Water Lily Garden
- [ ] C) Rose Garden

WHERE IN WASHINGTON?

The nation's capital, Washington, D.C., is home to some incredible sights. Many of the city's most important buildings, monuments, and museums are in a park called the National Mall. Millions of tourists visit the park every year.

Mia, Tom, and Grace are visiting the National Mall with their families. Find out which three sights each child visits by drawing their routes on the map below. Begin at the START points, and follow these instructions:

L = Turn left, R = Turn right, S = Go straight.

TIP: If the rights and lefts get confusing, rotate the page so that the map is facing the same direction as the child.

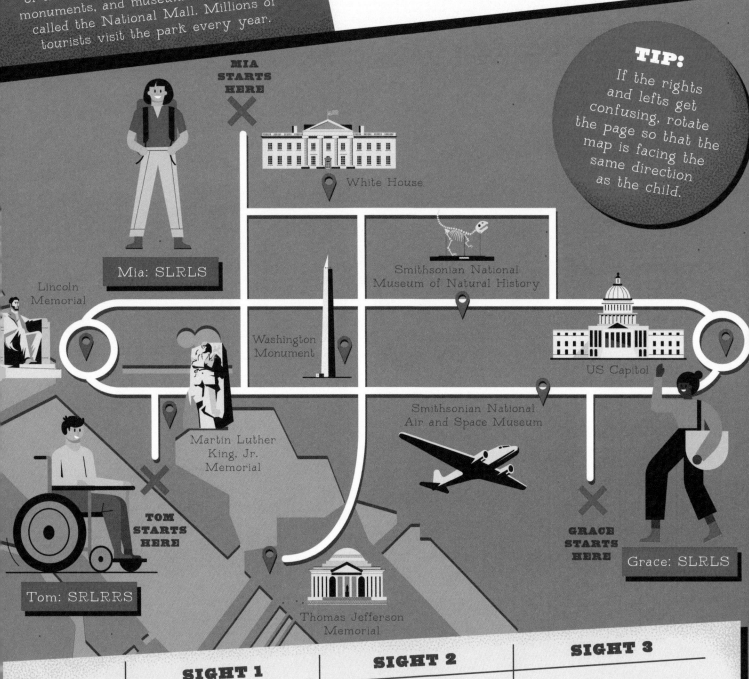

MIA STARTS HERE

White House

Lincoln Memorial

Mia: SLRLS

Smithsonian National Museum of Natural History

Washington Monument

US Capitol

Martin Luther King, Jr. Memorial

Smithsonian National Air and Space Museum

TOM STARTS HERE

GRACE STARTS HERE

Grace: SLRLS

Tom: SRLRRS

Thomas Jefferson Memorial

	SIGHT 1	SIGHT 2	SIGHT 3
Tom			
Grace			
Mia			

A-MAZE-ING EVERGLADES

THE EVERGLADES, ALSO KNOWN AS THE RIVER OF GRASS, IS A HUGE WETLAND IN SOUTHERN FLORIDA. MUCH OF IT IS COVERED BY SAW GRASS—A PLANT THAT GROWS IN WATER. VISITORS COME HERE TO ADMIRE THE HUGE VARIETY OF PLANT AND ANIMAL LIFE, INCLUDING AMERICAN ALLIGATORS.

CAN YOU FIND A PATH THROUGH THE SAW GRASS THAT AVOIDS THE ALLIGATORS?

START

END

THE LITTLE ISLANDS IN THE EVERGLADES ARE CALLED "HAMMOCKS."

LAND of FIRE

HAWAI`I IS FILLED WITH MANY INCREDIBLE MARVELS, INCLUDING HAWAI`I VOLCANOES NATIONAL PARK, WHICH IS HOME TO TWO OF THE WORLD'S MOST ACTIVE VOLCANOES—KĪLAUEA AND MAUNA LOA. KĪLAUEA HAS BEEN SPEWING LAVA NEARLY CONTINUOUSLY SINCE 1983!

IN HAWAIIAN MYTH AND CULTURE, THE STEAMING CRATER OF KĪLAUEA IS THE HOME OF PELE, THE GODDESS OF FIRE AND VOLCANOES. WHAT DO YOU THINK PELE MIGHT LOOK LIKE? DRAW HER IN THE SPACE BELOW. MAYBE HER HAIR COULD BE PLUMES OF SMOKE OR STREAMS OF RED-HOT LAVA!

HERE COMES THE SUN!

Cadillac Mountain, in Acadia National Park, in Maine, is the highest point on the east coast of America. In winter, it's the very first place in the whole of the United States to see the sun rise, and every morning people gather on the mountaintop to watch.

Imagine you're visiting the park and want to get up early to see the sunrise. Use the timings to work out what time you need to set your alarm for. The sun rises at 6:30 a.m. Don't be late!

Shower—20 minutes

Brush teeth—5 minutes

Get dressed—5 minutes

Drive to parking lot—30 minutes

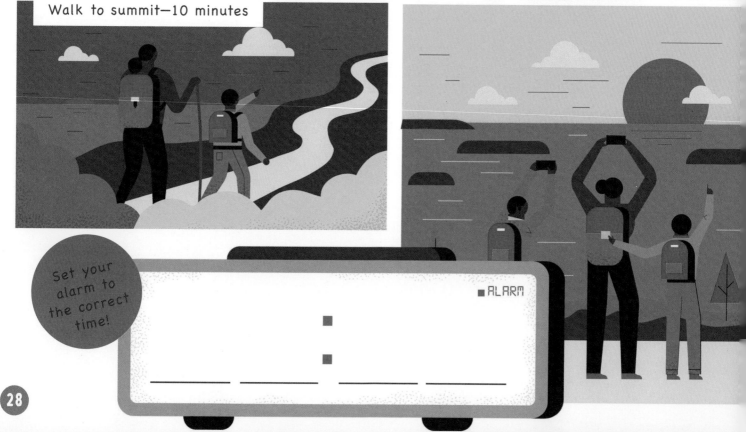

Walk to summit—10 minutes

Set your alarm to the correct time!

ALARM

SPECTACULAR SKYSCRAPERS

NEW YORK CITY IS THE HOME OF THE SKYSCRAPER! THERE ARE MORE OF THESE SUPER-TALL BUILDINGS HERE THAN ANYWHERE ELSE IN THE US.

TAKE A LOOK AT THESE FAMOUS NEW YORK SKYSCRAPERS. FOR A SHORT TIME, ONE OF THEM WAS THE TALLEST BUILDING IN THE WORLD—BUT WHICH ONE WAS IT? CROSS OUT THE SKYSCRAPERS THAT MATCH THE CLUES, THEN CIRCLE THE ONE SKYSCRAPER THAT REMAINS.

STEINWAY TOWER
HEIGHT: 1,428 FEET
BUILT: 2021
THINNEST SKYSCRAPER IN THE WORLD!

METLIFE BUILDING
HEIGHT: 808 FEET
BUILT: 1963

CHRYSLER BUILDING
HEIGHT: 1,046 FEET
BUILT: 1930

EMPIRE STATE BUILDING
HEIGHT: 1,250 FEET
BUILT: 1931

FLATIRON BUILDING
HEIGHT: 285 FEET
BUILT: 1902

NEW YORK LIFE BUILDING
HEIGHT: 615 FEET
BUILT: 1928
COVERED IN 25,000 GOLD-LEAF TILES

ONE WORLD TRADE CENTER
HEIGHT: 1,776 FEET
BUILT: 2014
TALLEST IN THE USA!

WOOLWORTH BUILDING
HEIGHT: 792 FEET
BUILT: 1913

CLUES:

1. THE SKYSCRAPER WAS BUILT BEFORE THE YEAR 2000.

2. THE SKYSCRAPER IS NOT TRIANGULAR.

3. THE FIRST NUMBER OF THE SKYSCRAPER'S HEIGHT IS AN ODD NUMBER.

4. THE SKYSCRAPER IS MORE THAN 1,000 FEET HIGH.

5. THE FIRST LETTER OF ITS NAME IS NOT A VOWEL (A, E, I, O, U).

DEATH VALLEY TRUE OR FALSE?

DEATH VALLEY, IN THE MOJAVE DESERT, IS ONE OF THE HOTTEST AND DRIEST PLACES ON EARTH. VISITORS CAN HIKE, CAMP, CYCLE, STARGAZE, TAKE GUIDED TOURS, AND MUCH MORE. READ THESE STATEMENTS ABOUT DEATH VALLEY, AND DECIDE IF EACH ONE IS TRUE OR FALSE. CIRCLE YOUR ANSWERS.

1. DEATH VALLEY IS IN THE STATE OF DELAWARE.

TRUE / FALSE

2. DEATH VALLEY CONTAINS THE LOWEST PLACE IN THE UNITED STATES.

TRUE / FALSE

3. COFFIN CANYON, FUNERAL MOUNTAINS, AND LAST CHANCE RANGE ARE ALL NAMES YOU'LL FIND ON A MAP OF DEATH VALLEY.

TRUE / FALSE

4. IT NEVER RAINS IN DEATH VALLEY.

TRUE / FALSE

5. MANATEES, FLORIDA PANTHERS, AND BROWN BEARS ALL LIVE IN DEATH VALLEY.

TRUE / FALSE

6. SEVERAL SCENES FROM THE STAR WARS MOVIES WERE SHOT IN DEATH VALLEY.

TRUE / FALSE

7. THE HIGHEST TEMPERATURE EVER RECORDED IN DEATH VALLEY WAS 434° FAHRENHEIT— AS HOT AS AN OVEN!

TRUE / FALSE

8. KANGAROO RATS IN DEATH VALLEY CAN GO THEIR WHOLE LIVES WITHOUT DRINKING WATER.

TRUE / FALSE

SUDOKU UNDER THE SEA

Florida's Coral Reef is one of the planet's largest barrier reefs, stretching for almost 350 miles. It's the only coral reef system in the continental US, and this magical underwater world is home to many delicate corals and other sea creatures.

Complete the sudoku puzzle by filling each square with a picture of a coral, a starfish, a loggerhead turtle, or a butterfly fish. Each row, column, and mini grid of four squares must contain all four creatures.

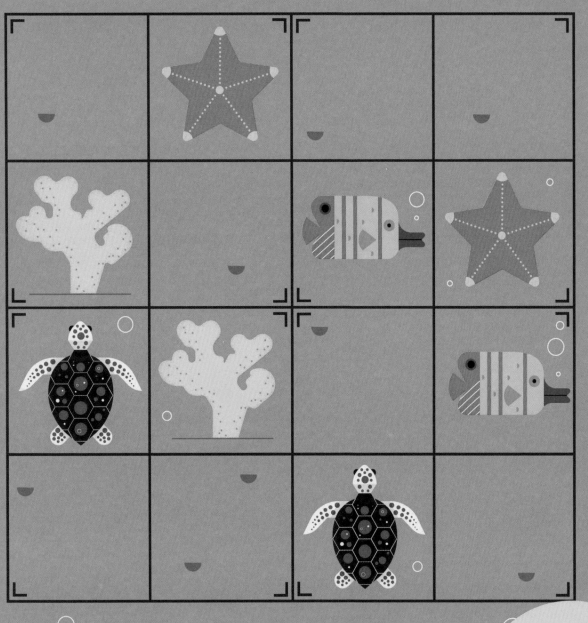

Visitors can experience this underwater treasure in many ways, from snorkeling in the shallows, to boat tours and deep-sea diving.

BACK IN TIME TEST

THE US IS HOME TO MANY AMAZING MUSEUMS, INCLUDING COLONIAL WILLIAMSBURG IN VIRGINIA—THE LARGEST LIVING HISTORY MUSEUM IN THE WORLD. VISITORS CAN EXPLORE HISTORIC BUILDINGS, MEET COSTUMED CHARACTERS, AND DISCOVER HOW PEOPLE LIVED AND WORKED IN 18TH-CENTURY AMERICA.

COLONIAL WILLIAMSBURG

THE OBJECTS BELOW ARE ALL THINGS THAT 18TH-CENTURY AMERICANS MIGHT HAVE WORN, OR USED, AT THAT TIME. STUDY THE EIGHT PICTURES FOR ONE MINUTE, THEN COVER THEM UP WITH A PIECE OF PAPER, AND WRITE DOWN AS MANY AS YOU CAN REMEMBER AT THE BOTTOM OF THE PAGE.

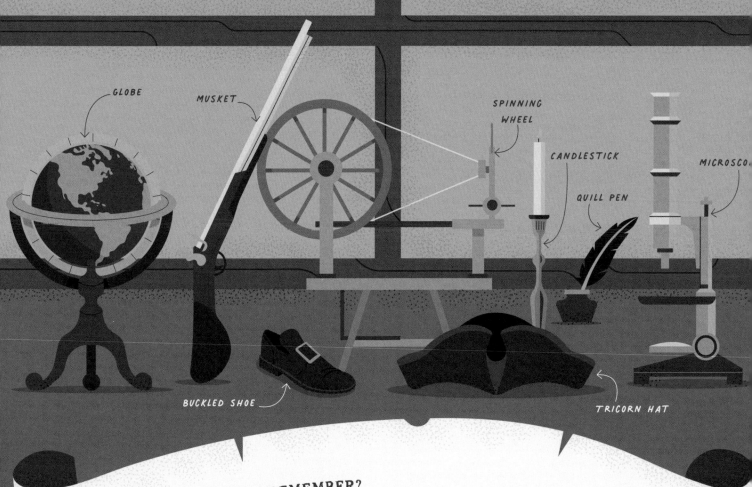

GLOBE

MUSKET

SPINNING WHEEL

CANDLESTICK

QUILL PEN

MICROSCO...

BUCKLED SHOE

TRICORN HAT

WHICH ITEMS CAN YOU REMEMBER?

FINDERS KEEPERS

Crater of Diamonds State Park, in Murfreesboro, Arkansas, is the only diamond mine in the world where you are allowed to hunt for precious gems and keep anything you find! Since 1972, visitors have dug up amethysts, garnets, and over 33,000 diamonds.

Imagine you are visiting the park and find a sparkling diamond the size of a dime! Write a diary entry about your discovery. What will you do with your million-dollar diamond?

WONDERFUL WILDFLOWERS

Every spring, many prairies, forests, deserts, meadows, and mountain slopes come alive with dazzling displays of wildflowers. People from all over travel to these spots to witness the flowers in bloom. In each row of wildflowers below, circle the one that's different from all the rest.

Indian paintbrush

Glacier National Park in Montana is one of the best places in the country to see wildflowers, including Indian paintbrush.

Dwarf iris

Great Smoky Mountains National Park, in Tennessee and North Carolina, has so many wildflowers it's nicknamed the "Wildflower National Park." A common flower found here is the dwarf iris.

California poppy

Each spring, Antelope Valley in California is carpeted by golden California poppies.

Texas bluebonnet

In parts of Texas, spring sees fields covered in bluebonnets—the official state flower.

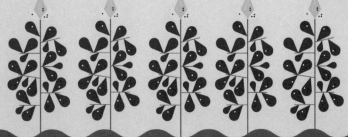

Saguaro cactus

At Saguaro National Park in Arizona, prickly saguaro cacti flower in the desert.

DINO DIG

DINOSAURS DIED OUT MANY MILLIONS OF YEARS AGO, BUT THE UNITED STATES IS ONE OF THE BEST PLACES ON THE PLANET FOR FINDING THEIR REMAINS—FOSSILIZED BONES, FOOTPRINTS, TEETH, EGGS, EVEN POOP! SOME OF THE MOST FAMOUS FOSSIL SITES ARE IN UTAH, WYOMING, COLORADO, MONTANA, AND TEXAS. MANY STATES HAVE MUSEUMS AND PARKS THAT YOU CAN VISIT TO SEE FOSSILS UP CLOSE AND LEARN MORE.

FIND AND CIRCLE 10 BONES SHAPED LIKE THIS ONE IN THE SCENE BELOW:

SOME ARE SMALLER THAN OTHERS!

RECORD BREAKER OR RECORD FAKER?

Some of these record-breaking sights are real-life marvels, and some are made up. Can you figure out which is which? Read the descriptions and locations carefully, then circle the three fakes.

1. Tallest sand dune in North America—Bruneau Dunes State Park, Idaho

BREAKER OR FAKER?

2. Largest train station in the world—Grand Central Station, New York

BREAKER OR FAKER?

3. Largest glacier in North America—Sunshine Glacier, Georgia

BREAKER OR FAKER?

4. Tallest skyscraper in the world—Dubai City, North Dakota

BREAKER OR FAKER?

5. Oldest operating lighthouse in the United States—Sandy Hook Lighthouse, New Jersey

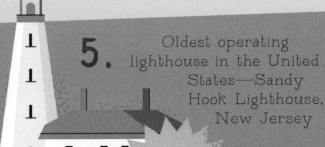

BREAKER OR FAKER?

6. Longest coral reef in North America—Million Mile Beach, Oklahoma

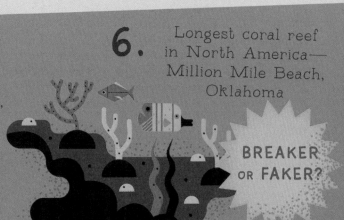

BREAKER OR FAKER?

WEIRD AND WONDERFUL

All over the US there are thrilling things to see, from beautiful natural wonders to impressive man-made structures. But did you know there are also plenty of strange and silly sights, too? Take a look at these weird and wonderful examples of real roadside attractions that people love to visit ...

CADILLAC RANCH
Amarillo, Texas

Ten vintage Cadillac cars, half-buried in the ground, make up this public art installation. Visitors can take pictures by the cars, or even add their own mark in paint.

WORLD'S LARGEST BALL OF PAINT
Alexandria, Indiana

This oddball marvel started out as a baseball, but after tens of thousands of coats of paint, it now weighs about the same as a rhino!

W'EEL TURTLE
Dunseith, North Dakota

Think up an unusual attraction of your own, and draw it here.

This giant turtle sculpture is made from over 2,000 old wheel rims!

MAJESTIC MISSISSIPPI

THE MIGHTY MISSISSIPPI RIVER IS THE SECOND LONGEST RIVER IN THE US, AFTER THE MISSOURI RIVER. IT IS HOME TO LOTS OF ANIMALS, AND IT PROVIDES WATER TO MANY PEOPLE. FISHING AND RIDING ON STEAMBOATS ARE POPULAR ACTIVITIES TO TRY HERE.

THE RIVER PASSES THOUGH TEN STATES ON ITS 2,340-MILE JOURNEY TO THE ATLANTIC OCEAN. FILL IN THE CROSSWORD GRID WITH THE NAMES OF THE STATES.

4 LETTERS
IOWA

8 LETTERS
ILLINOIS
MISSOURI
ARKANSAS
KENTUCKY

9 LETTERS
LOUISIANA
MINNESOTA
TENNESSEE
WISCONSIN

11 LETTERS
MISSISSIPPI

IT TAKES AROUND 90 DAYS FOR A DROP OF WATER TO TRAVEL FROM ONE END OF THE RIVER TO THE OTHER.

WATER, WATER, EVERYWHERE

THROUGHOUT THE US YOU CAN FIND MANY FAMOUS LAKES, RIVERS, AND GLACIERS. CRACK THE CODES TO FIND THE NAMES OF THREE NATIONAL PARKS THAT PROTECT SOME OF THE COUNTRY'S MOST IMPRESSIVE WATERY WONDERS.

1. CROSS OUT THE RED AND BLUE LETTERS TO UNCOVER THE NAME OF A NATIONAL PARK IN OREGON WHERE YOU CAN FIND THE DEEPEST LAKE IN THE US. THE LAKE WAS FORMED FROM A COLLAPSED VOLCANO.

S P T C K R Z L A T B E K R   R O L G A E K H Y E

_____

_____

2. CROSS OUT ALL THE X'S, Y'S, AND Z'S TO FIND THE NAME OF A NATIONAL PARK IN WEST VIRGINIA THAT INCLUDES A STRETCH OF ONE OF THE OLDEST RIVERS IN NORTH AMERICA.

X N Z E X Y W Z   Y Z R Y I V X E Y Z R   Z G Y O X Y R Z G Y X E Y

_____

_____

3. CROSS OUT ALL THE GREEN LETTERS AND ALL OF THE X'S TO FIND THE NAME OF A NATIONAL PARK IN ALASKA THAT IS HOME TO SOME OF THE WORLD'S LONGEST AND LARGEST GLACIERS.

X F W R T A N X G R X E X L L E   S P X S T   E H L I X A R S

_____

_____

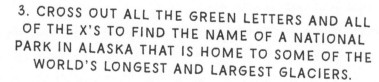

Next in Line

Lake Pontchartrain Causeway in Louisiana is a marvel of engineering. At almost 24 miles long, it's the longest bridge in the US. For a stretch of 8 miles, there's no land in sight at all!

Study the four lines of traffic, below. For each line, work out which vehicle comes next in the pattern, and describe or draw it in the space at the bottom of the page.

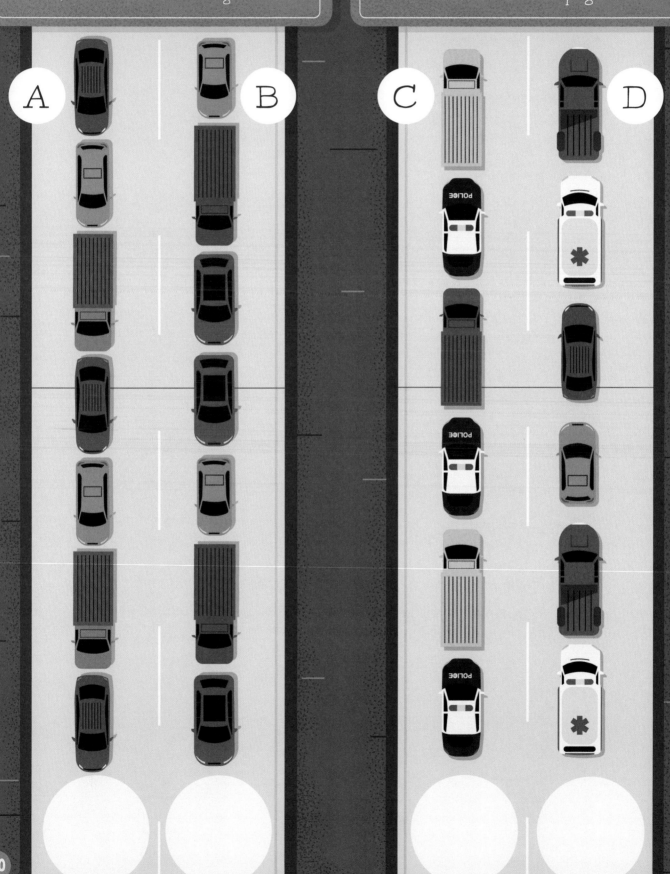

Hoover Dam Makeover

The Hoover Dam, on the border of Arizona and Nevada, was built in the 1930s to generate hydroelectric power. The enormous structure is 726 feet tall, and its base is as thick as two football fields placed end to end!

Use your imagination to give the dam a makeover. For example, you could draw colorful plants growing up it, turn it into the world's biggest climbing wall, or draw a wiggly waterslide running from top to bottom—wheeeeee!

It's estimated that the concrete in the dam will last for 10,000 years.

The amount of concrete used in the dam could pave a highway from San Francisco to New York City!

Glow Wild

The Great Smoky Mountains straddle
the border of North Carolina and
Tennessee. For a few weeks every year, between
May and June, the forests of these mountains come alight
with a magical twinkling display. The spectacle is
created by tens of thousands of fireflies flashing
in harmony, all at exactly the same time.

Each type of firefly has different flash
patterns, so males and females of the same
type can find each other. Follow the glowing
trails of these male fireflies to see which
one leads to the female firefly.

STALACTITE SUMS

COPY THESE CLUSTERS OF STALACTITES ONTO THE CEILINGS OF THE THREE CAVES BELOW, SO THAT EACH CAVE HAS 20 STALACTITES IN TOTAL. ONE OF THE CLUSTERS HAS BEEN DRAWN ON FOR YOU.

MAMMOTH CAVE, IN KENTUCKY, IS THE WORLD'S LONGEST CAVE SYSTEM. OVER 400 MILES OF PASSAGES HAVE BEEN EXPLORED—SO FAR!

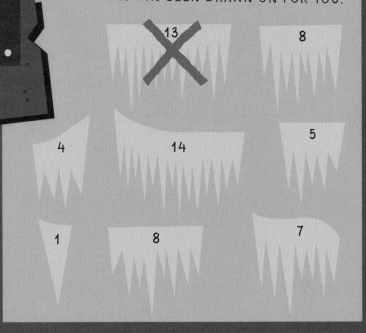

13   8

4   14   5

1   8   7

13

GOLDEN GATE PAIRS

The Golden Gate Bridge was built in 1937 to link the city of San Francisco to the hills of Marin County, in California. It is thought to be the most photographed bridge in the world, and its famous red-orange color is called "International Orange."

In the picture of the Golden Gate Bridge below, find and circle the boat, vehicle, and hot-air balloon without a match.

ESCAPE FROM ALCATRAZ!

The federal prison on Alcatraz Island in the middle of San Francisco Bay, in California, was said to be the most escape-proof prison in the United States. Up until 1963, when the prison closed, not a single escape attempt from "The Rock" proved successful. Today, tourists can visit the island and see the empty cells.

Using the information below, can you crack the three-number combination code on the padlock and escape from Alcatraz? The code uses the numbers 1 to 9.

482 — two of the numbers are correct and in the right place.

235 — none of the numbers are correct.

652 — one number is correct, but it's in the wrong place.

Write the correct code in the spaces on the padlock.

ROCK STARS

Take a look at these geological marvels. Most of them are in the US, but not all! Unscramble the anagrams to reveal either the name of a state, or the name of another country. Then circle the five American wonders.

Giant's Causeway
THERNORN LANIRED

Bryce Canyon National Park
ATHU

Devils Tower
WOMINGY

Uluru
ALARAUSTI

Chimney Rock
ASKABREN

Arches National Park
UTHA

Stone Forest of Shilin
HINAC

Antelope Canyon
ORAZINA

METEOR
WORD LADDER

Arizona's Meteor Crater was formed around 50,000 years ago, when a giant meteorite hit the Earth at 40,000 miles per hour. The massive crater it created is almost a mile wide!

Complete this word ladder to turn "ROCK" into "HOLE." Start at the top and work your way down, changing one letter at each step to make a new word. The clues will help you.

Here's an example:

CAT → COT → DOT → DOG

ROCK

_ _ _ _   CLUE: Something you wear on your foot

_ _ _ _   CLUE: Feeling ill

_ _ _ _   CLUE: A fiber spun by silkworms

_ _ _ _   CLUE: A white liquid that you might drink

_ _ _ _   CLUE: A measurement of distance

_ _ _ _   CLUE: A large number of things put on top of each other

_ _ _ _   CLUE: A long, thin stick

HOLE

TIMES SQUARE I-SPY

BUSTLING CROWDS, FLASHING NEON SIGNS, AND BIG, BRIGHT BILLBOARDS—WELCOME TO TIMES SQUARE IN NEW YORK CITY! THIS FAMOUS SQUARE ATTRACTS ABOUT 50 MILLION VISITORS EVERY YEAR, MORE THAN ANY OTHER AMERICAN ATTRACTION.

STUDY THE BUSY SCENE BELOW, AND FIND AND CIRCLE THESE THINGS:

- 2 BLUE BAGS
- A DOG
- 2 RED TIES
- A BLUE BASEBALL CAP
- A CLOCK
- A HOT DOG
- A BILLBOARD ADVERTISING A SHOE
- A "NO LEFT TURN" STREET SIGN

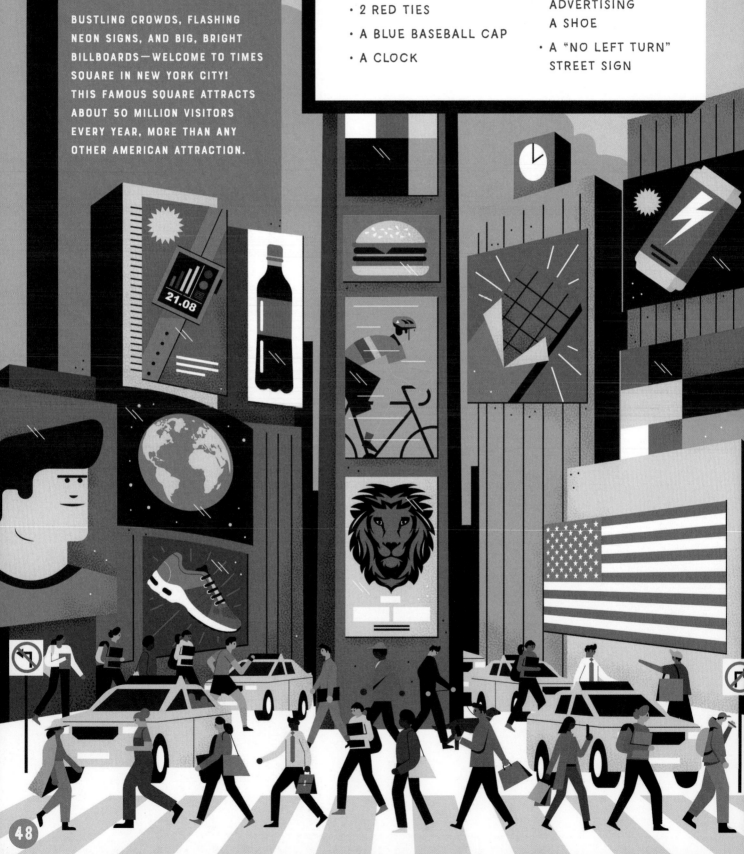

WELCOME TO HOLLYWOOD!

COLOR IN THE FAMOUS SIGN TO GIVE IT A MAKEOVER.

THE HOLLYWOOD SIGN IS A FAMOUS LANDMARK OVERLOOKING LOS ANGELES—THE CITY OF MOVIES, FAME, AND FORTUNE! EACH OF THE ENORMOUS LETTERS IS 45 FEET TALL.

HOLLYWOOD

SPOT THE DIFFERENCE
IN CARLSBAD CAVERNS

SUMMERTIME VISITORS TO CARLSBAD CAVERNS IN NEW MEXICO GATHER AT SUNSET TO WATCH AN AMAZING SIGHT—HUNDREDS OF THOUSANDS OF BRAZILIAN FREE-TAILED BATS STREAMING OUT OF A CAVE. THE LITTLE BATS DART AND DIVE IN THE NIGHT SKY, HUNTING FOR MOTHS AND OTHER TASTY INSECTS TO EAT.

FIND AND CIRCLE EIGHT DIFFERENCES BETWEEN THE TWO PICTURES OF CARLSBAD CAVERN BELOW.

Star to Star

The Mauna Kea Observatories in Hawai'i are home to some of the biggest telescopes in the world, used to study distant stars and planets.

Connect the dots from a to g, to reveal a well-known constellation (pattern of stars) called the Big Dipper. Then create your own constellation by connecting some of the other stars in the sky. What shape will it be? It could be an object, an animal, or something else.

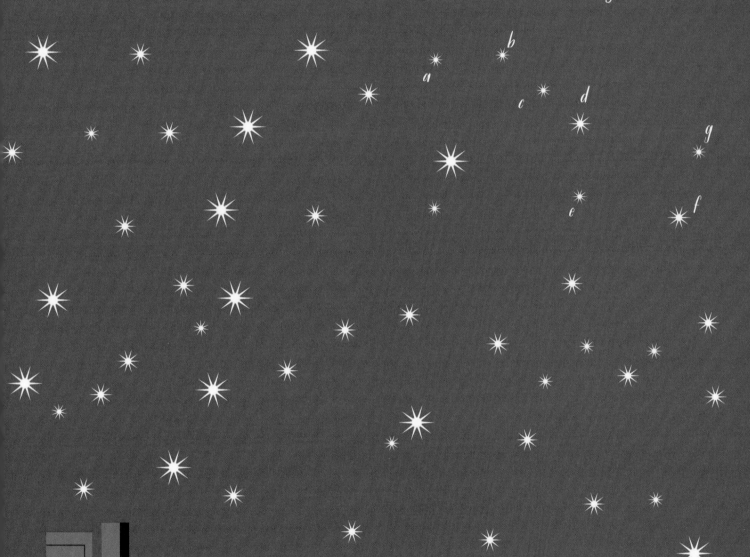

My constellation is called:

WHO, WHAT, WHERE?

Some marvels of nature can only be seen at certain times of the year. The pictures below show three children, three locations, and three beautiful, seasonal sights. Read the clues and work out which spectacle each child saw, and where they saw it. Fill in the grid at the bottom of the page with the answers.

New England is made up of six states: Connecticut, Maine, Massachusetts, New Hampshire, Rhode Island, and Vermont.

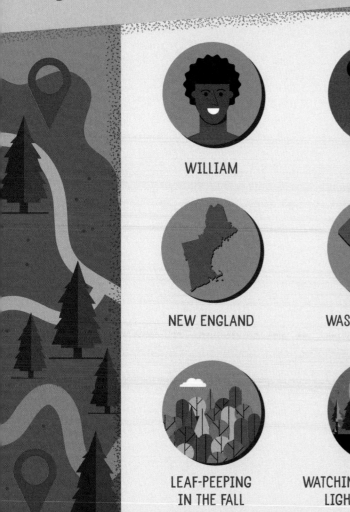

WILLIAM

EVELYN

ALICIA

NEW ENGLAND

WASHINGTON, D.C.

ALASKA

LEAF-PEEPING IN THE FALL

WATCHING THE NORTHERN LIGHTS IN WINTER

ADMIRING THE CHERRY BLOSSOMS IN SPRING

NAME	LOCATION	SIGHT
ALICIA		
WILLIAM		
EVELYN		

CLUES:

1. Alicia went to Alaska.

2. The person who went leaf-peeping in New England was not a girl.

3. The person who went to Washington, D.C., did not see the northern lights.

52

INDIANAPOLIS NUMBER SEARCH

The Indianapolis Motor Speedway, in Speedway, Indiana, is the largest sports venue in the world. Its famous racetrack is so big it could fit fourteen White Houses inside! Spectators come here to watch superfast cars race around the track.

Find and circle the race car numbers hidden inside the grid. The numbers can go up, down, across, or diagonally.

```
0 8 4 2
9 1 2 7 3 5
1 3 4 0 9 0
7 8 2 7 1 2
0 7 1 6 4 4 9 8
0 6 2 7 3 1 1 3
9 4 0 0 8 9
1 9 7 4 7 6
3 2 7 4 7 3
1 9 0 0
```

Every year, the racetrack hosts the famous Indy 500 race.

53

At the Library

There are more than 170 million items and about 838 miles of bookshelves at the Library of Congress in Washington, D.C. It's the largest library in the world!

Help the librarian find the book she is searching for, using the information below. When you find the book, circle it. Good luck!

- It is on the shelf that is immediately above the shelf that is two shelves below the top shelf.

- It is one book to the left of a book that is three books to the right of a book that is yellow.

- It is not next to a green book.

Home Sweet Home

Throughout the US you can find many famous historic homes. These buildings show the fashions and styles of the past. Some are open to the public, and others are simply popular photo opportunities.

Read the descriptions of the famous historic American homes below, then draw lines to match them to the correct name and picture. Lastly, circle the home you'd most like to live in.

8 SPRUCE STREET
NEW YORK

TAOS PUEBLO
NEW MEXICO

BILTMORE ESTATE
NORTH CAROLINA

FALLINGWATER
PENNSYLVANIA

PAINTED LADIES
CALIFORNIA

DESCRIPTIONS:

1.
These beautiful adobe mud brick houses are part of a Native American pueblo. They were built over 600 years ago.

2.
This is the largest home in America, built in the 1890s by George Vanderbilt in the style of a French chateau.

3.
This row of colorful Victorian houses is a famous sight in California.

4.
Architect Frank Lloyd Wright built this modern house over a waterfall in 1935.

5.
This crinkly skyscraper was designed by architect Frank Gehry. Inside are about 900 apartments and a school!

TIME TRAVEL

Have you heard of time capsules? These are containers that are buried in the ground and are meant to be opened in the future. Inside, people place objects that show what life is like in their time. The world's largest time capsule is buried in Seward, Nebraska. It was sealed in 1975 and will be opened in 2025. The vault, filled with 5,000 items, was created by Harold Davisson to show his grandchildren what life was like in the 1970s.

Imagine you are creating a time capsule. Use the prompts below to draw or write what you would put in it.

A POPULAR TOY

AN ITEM OF CLOTHING

SOMETHING UNEXPECTED

A PHOTOGRAPH OF YOU

A USEFUL MACHINE PEOPLE HAVE IN THEIR HOMES

SOMETHING THAT HAS JUST BEEN INVENTED

A TYPE OF TRANSPORTATION

YEAR CAPSULE SHOULD BE OPENED:

HOMETOWN MARVEL

YOU DON'T HAVE TO TRAVEL TO A FAMOUS CITY OR
A BEAUTIFUL NATIONAL PARK TO FIND A MARVEL OF THE USA.

THINK OF SOMETHING AMAZING CLOSE TO WHERE YOU LIVE—
IT COULD BE A COOL BUILDING OR AN INTERESTING MONUMENT,
A BEAUTIFUL TREE OR A TINY FLOWER. DRAW IT HERE, AND SAY
WHY IT DESERVES ITS PLACE ON A LIST OF MARVELS OF THE USA.

PLACE:

THIS IS A MARVEL OF THE USA BECAUSE:

ANSWERS

PAGE 7: WHERE AM I?
Cloud Gate: Illinois
Mauna Kea Observatories: Hawaiʻi
Sandy Hook Lighthouse: New Jersey
Biltmore Estate: North Carolina
Chimney Rock: Nebraska
World's largest ball of paint: Indiana

PAGE 9: WHAT'S WRONG IN THE PARK?

PAGE 10: GREAT LAKES WORD SEARCH

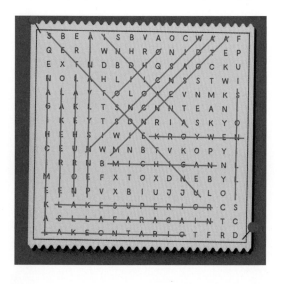

PAGE 11: MULTICOLOR MARVEL

PAGE 13: WHICH WONDER, WHICH CITY?
Brooklyn Bridge, New York City
Cloud Gate, Chicago
Gateway Arch, St. Louis
Space Needle, Seattle
Transamerica Pyramid, San Francisco

PAGE 14: CANYON MEMORY CHALLENGE
1. White
2. Four
3. Bald eagle, elk, bighorn sheep
4. Four

PAGE 15: MOUNTAIN MAZE

PAGE 17: ROLLER COASTER RIDERS

PAGE 18: TREE CODE CRACKER

1. Bristlecone pines
2. General Sherman
3. Hyperion

PAGE 21: FORT KNOX MAZE

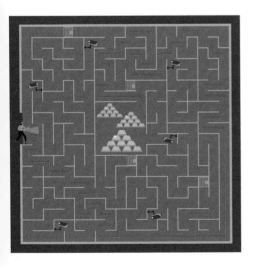

PAGE 22: GLACIER BAY HIDE-AND-SEEK

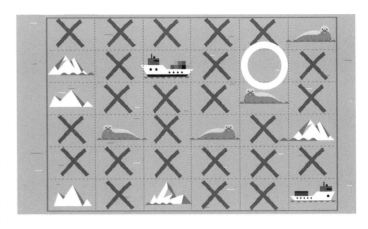

PAGE 23: NIAGARA FALLS UNSCRAMBLE

Maid of the Mist

PAGE 24: WHITE HOUSE QUIZ

1. C
2. A
3. B
4. B
5. C
6. A
7. C

PAGE 25: WHERE IN WASHINGTON?

Tom: Martin Luther King, Jr. Memorial, Washington Monument, Thomas Jefferson Memorial

Grace: Smithsonian National Air and Space Museum, Washington Monument, Lincoln Memorial

Mia: White House, Smithsonian National Museum of Natural History, US Capitol

PAGE 26: A-MAZE-ING EVERGLADES

PAGE 28: HERE COMES THE SUN!
5:20 a.m.

PAGE 29: SPECTACULAR SKYSCRAPERS
The Chrysler Building was the tallest building in the world from 1931 to 1932 when it was overtaken by the Empire State Building. Its architect added a spire at the last minute to beat its rivals!

PAGE 30: DEATH VALLEY TRUE OR FALSE?
1. False—it's in California.
2. True—Badwater Basin, an area within Death Valley, is 282 feet below sea level.
3. True.
4. False—its average rainfall each year is around 1.5 inches.
5. False—none of these animals live in Death Valley.
6. True—scenes from Episodes IV and VI were shot here.
7. False—the highest temperature was actually 134° F (still pretty hot!).
8. True—they get all the water they need from the seeds they eat.

PAGE 31: SUDOKU UNDER THE SEA

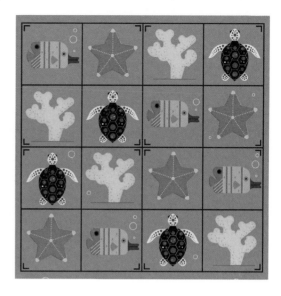

PAGE 34: WONDERFUL WILDFLOWERS

PAGE 35: DINO DIG

PAGE 36: RECORD BREAKER OR RECORD FAKER?

1. Record breaker—it's 470 feet tall.
2. Record breaker—it's the world's largest, by number of platforms.
3. Record faker—Georgia doesn't have any glaciers; it's not cold enough in the southern US.
4. Record faker—the world's tallest skyscraper is in Dubai in the UAE.
5. Record breaker—Sandy Hook Lighthouse was built in 1764.
6. Record faker—Oklahoma doesn't have any coral reefs because it doesn't have a coastline!

PAGE 38: MAJESTIC MISSISSIPPI

PAGE 39: WATER, WATER, EVERYWHERE

1. Crater Lake (1,943 feet deep)
2. New River Gorge
3. Wrangell St. Elias

PAGE 40: NEXT IN LINE

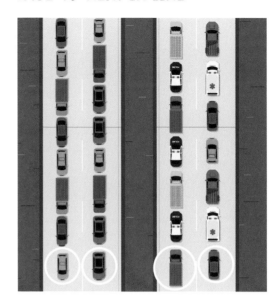

LANE 1: Orange car
LANE 2: Red car
LANE 3: Red truck
LANE 4: Blue car

PAGE 42: GLOW WILD

Trail B is the correct one.

PAGE 43: STALACTITE SUMS

The groups of stalactites that belong together are: 13 and 7; 14, 5, and 1; and 8, 8, and 4.

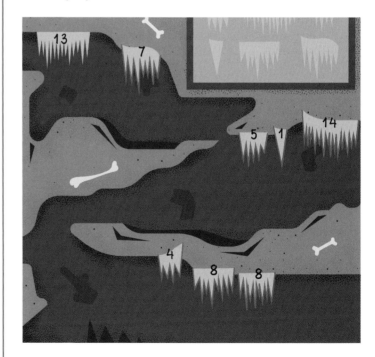

PAGE 44: GOLDEN GATE PAIRS

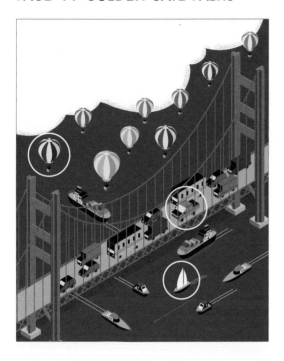

PAGE 45: ESCAPE FROM ALCATRAZ!

The code is 486.

PAGE 46: ROCK STARS

Giant's Causeway: Northern Ireland
Bryce Canyon National Park: Utah *
Devils Tower: Wyoming *
Uluru: Australia
Chimney Rock: Nebraska *
Arches National Park: Utah *
Stone Forest of Shilin: China
Antelope Canyon: Arizona *

PAGE 47: METEOR WORD LADDER

SOCK
SICK
SILK
MILK
MILE
PILE
POLE

PAGE 48: TIMES SQUARE I-SPY

PAGE 50: SPOT THE DIFFERENCE IN CARLSBAD CAVERNS

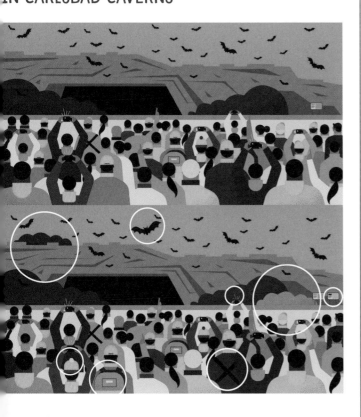

PAGE 51: STAR TO STAR

PAGE 52: WHO, WHAT, WHERE?

NAME	LOCATION	SIGHT
ALICIA	ALASKA	NORTHERN LIGHTS
WILLIAM	NEW ENGLAND	LEAF-PEEPING
EVELYN	WASHINGTON, D.C.	CHERRY BLOSSOMS

PAGE 53: INDIANAPOLIS NUMBER SEARCH

PAGE 54: AT THE LIBRARY

PAGE 55: HOME SWEET HOME

1. Taos Pueblo, New Mexico
2. Biltmore Estate, North Carolina
3. Painted Ladies, California
4. Fallingwater, Pennsylvania
5. 8 Spruce Street, New York

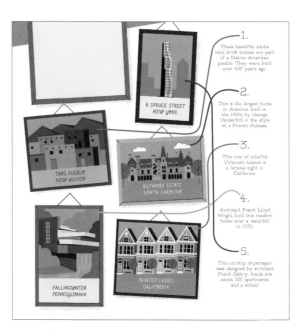

First American Edition 2022
Kane Miller, A Division of EDC Publishing

Marvels of the USA Activity Book © 2022 Quarto Publishing plc

For information contact:
Kane Miller, A Division of EDC Publishing
5402 S 122nd E Ave
Tulsa, OK 74146
www.kanemiller.com
www.myubam.com

Manufactured in Huizhou City, Guangdong, China. TT032022

ISBN: 978-1-68464-286-1

1 2 3 4 5 6 7 8 9 10